Primary
Word Work

BOOK 3

Louis Fidge
Sarah Lindsay

Collins Educational
An imprint of HarperCollinsPublishers

Published by Collins Educational
An imprint of HarperCollins*Publishers* Ltd
77-85 Fulham Palace Road
London W6 8JB

First published 1998
Reprinted 1999

ISBN 0 00 302488 1

Illustrations by Maggie Brand, Rob Englebright, Belinda Evans, Bethan Matthews,
Andrew Midgley.

British Library Cataloguing in Publication Data
A catalogue record for this book is available from the British Library.

Cover illustration: Bethan Matthews
Editor: Janet Swarbrick
Designer: Celia Hart

Printed by Scotprint, Musselburgh

Contents

UNIT 1 — Synonyms

Synonyms are words with **similar meanings.**
We need to choose the **most appropriate** word
which **best expresses** what we are trying to say.

I like to keep the books tidy. I get **irritated** when someone leaves them in a mess.

I thought Anna was my best friend. I was **upset** when she didn't invite me to her party.

I was **cross** when I was deliberately fouled just as I was about to score.

The man was **furious** when someone crashed into his new car.

The words in bold are all synonyms for **angry**, but they all have a **slightly different meaning**.

Remember to use a thesaurus when looking for synonyms.

Practice

Find and write down the ten pairs of synonyms.

| Set A | new | wander | aid | broad | start |
| | cunning | feeble | copy | strong | slim |

| Set B | weak | help | wide | sly | roam |
| | imitate | powerful | modern | slender | begin |

More to think about

Find the three words with similar meanings in each set.
Write down these synonyms.

1. <u>brave</u>   adult   <u>fearless</u>   attractive   <u>courageous</u>
2. snap   tell   inform   notice   notify
3. rough   harsh   argue   alarm   uneven
4. old   jolly   ancient   valuable   antique
5. special   remote   lonely   selfish   isolated

Now try these

1. Copy the sentences. Choose the best synonym for each.

   a) | snatched   seized   captured |

   The police _____ the thief who had escaped.
   The mugger _____ the old lady's handbag.
   The eagle _____ the mouse in its claws.

   b) | adjust   change   alter |

   My trousers were too long so my mum
   had to _____ them.
   A chameleon can _____ its colour
   to match its surroundings.
   You can usually _____ the colour
   on a TV set with its remote control.

2. Make up sentences to show you know the difference in
   meaning between the three synonyms in each set.
   a) gobble nibble devour   b) pour spill drip
   c) kind helpful generous   d) examine notice recognise

UNIT 2

Soft c and soft g

Read these words aloud and listen to the different sound the **c** makes.

city

mice

clown

If the **c** sounds **s**, as in **c**ity or mi**c**e, we say it is a **soft c**.
The letter **c** is usually soft when followed by an **i**, **e** or **y**.

Read these words aloud and listen to the different sound the **g** makes.

giraffe

pa**g**e

goat

If the **g** sounds **j**, as in **g**iraffe or pa**g**e, we say it is a **soft g**.

Practice

Copy these words. Underline those with a soft **c** or **g**.
Circle those with a hard **c** or **g**.

angel   game   garden   circus

cereal   rice   DANGER

magic   clock   gypsy   clarinet   face

accident   dance   vegetable

More to think about

Copy the table. Write five words in each column.
The pictures may help you get started.

age	ace	nge	ice

Now try these

Find nine words with either a
soft c or soft g in the wordsearch.

e	x	c	e	p	t	c
n	c	a	g	e	m	i
c	i	t	y	n	f	r
o	k	l	m	c	d	c
t	m	a	g	i	c	u
a	n	g	e	l	s	i
p	c	y	g	n	e	t

Dialogue words and adverbs

Dialogue words are verbs that express the way we **say** things – like **said, replied, shouted. Adverbs** are words that tell us **more about verbs.** Adverbs often tell us **how** something was done.

"Where did you get it?" she asked **accusingly**.

"Where did you get it?" she gasped **admiringly**.

"Where did you get it?" she laughed **scornfully**.

"Where did you get it?" she exclaimed **gratefully**.

Practice

Copy the sentences. Choose the best adverb to complete each one.

1. We shout _____ (loudly/fondly).

2. We laugh _____ (sadly/happily).

3. We whisper _____ (bravely/quietly).

4. We weep _____ (sadly/simply).

5. We answer _____ (kindly/correctly).

6. We sing _____ (tunefully/painfully).

7. We argue _____ (quietly/noisily).

More to think about

Copy the sentences. Choose the most suitable adverb from the box to complete each one.

| breathlessly | fondly | angrily | hopefully | sleepily |
| haltingly | | honestly | | fiercely |

1. "It's nearly three in the morning," Tom yawned __sleepily__.
2. "You are a good daughter," Ann's mother said _____.
3. "Get away from me," the man snarled _____.
4. "I've run all the way home," gasped Sam _____.
5. "It's a g…g…g…ghost!" Tom stammered _____.
6. "Please may I come?" the child asked _____.
7. "I didn't do it," the suspect declared _____.
8. "That vacuum cleaner you sold me is rubbish!" complained the lady _____.

Now try these

Think of an adverb that you could use with each of these dialogue words to make them more interesting.

1. You can sigh __wearily__.
2. You can chuckle _____.
3. You can grumble _____.
4. You can mutter _____.
5. You can yell _____.
6. You can explain _____.
7. You can insist _____.
8. You can ask _____.

9

Plurals

There are several ways of making words **plural**.

cat   cat**s**

We just add **s** to most words.

dish   dish**es**

We add **es** to most words ending in **s**, **x**, **sh** and **ch**.

thie**f**   thie**ves**

We drop the last letter and add **ves** to most words ending in **f**.

bab**y**   bab**ies**

We change the **y** to **i** and add **es** to most words ending in **y** with a consonant before it.

Practice

Write the labels for the pictures.

1. four (fly) – four flies

2. three (puppy)

3. five (leaf)

4. six (banana)

5. two (donkey)

6. two (church)

More to think about

Copy the sentences. Change the underlined words into their plural form.

1. The <u>lily</u> in the <u>vase</u> filled the room with scent.

2. There were lots of <u>activity</u> and <u>thing</u> to do.

3. The <u>leaf</u> fell from the <u>tree</u> as the days got colder.

4. Sophie looked for the <u>address</u> in the phone book.

5. The <u>fox</u> hid behind the <u>bush</u> watching the people.

6. When the fire <u>bell</u> sounded, the <u>class</u> went outside sensibly.

7. The <u>artist</u> had painted excellent <u>picture</u> for the exhibition.

Now try these

1. Write the plural of each of these nouns.
   a) country   b) church   c) father
   d) hobby   e) roof   f) box
   g) whistle   h) dish   i) lady
   j) shelf   k) pulley   l) lamb

2. Use at least eight of the plurals you have made in some sentences of your own.

Root words

Sometimes we can group words according to their **roots** (origins).

Signum is the Latin word for a **sign**. Look at some of the words that come from it.

What do you notice about the sound of the **g** in the words?

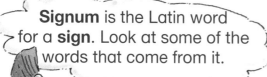

sign	**sign**al
signature	**sign**ify
re**sign**	de**sign**

The words can often be identified as they have the **same word** (or part of the word) **in common**.

Practice

Copy these words. Write the root word from which each comes.

1. disappearance – *appear*
2. colouring
3. pressure
4. recovery
5. helpful
6. continued
7. increased
8. likely
9. washing
10. direction
11. attractive
12. television

More to think about

Find a word from each set that has the same root word.
Write them like this: <u>detect</u>   <u>detective</u>   <u>detection</u>

Set A	<u>detect</u> format special vary statue graph telescope cap fact medic

Set B	medical factory perform capital various especially <u>detective</u> graphics television statement

Set C	captain medicine estate speciality manufacture information variety <u>detection</u> paragraph telephone

Now try these

1. Find the two words in the box that come from each root word.

> anagram   expedition   dental   astrology
> grammar   disaster   sympathy   autograph
> pathetic   indent   pedestrian   autobiography

   a) **auto** (from Greek, meaning *self*)

   b) **pathos** (from Greek, meaning *feeling*)

   c) **gramma** (from Greek, meaning *written*)

   d) **aster** (from Latin, meaning *star*)

   e) **pedis** (from Latin, meaning *foot*)

   f) **dentis** (from Latin, meaning *tooth*)

2. Think of some more words with the same roots as the pairs above.

Prefixes (1)

Prefixes change the **meanings** of **words** in a particular way.

Atlantic = the ocean separating the Americas and Europe and Africa

transatlantic = anything that crosses the Atlantic ocean

plane = an aeroplane

biplane = a type of aeroplane with two sets of wings

Practice

Copy these words. Take off the prefixes. Write the root word from which each word comes.

1. telephone – phone
2. bicycle
3. transform
4. circumnavigate
5. autobiography
6. transplant
7. bimonthly

More to think about

Decide which prefix to use to complete each word. Use a dictionary to help.

auto	bi	trans	tele	circum

1. _____phone

2. _____annual

3. _____graph

4. _____plane

5. _____action

6. _____scope

7. _____scribe

8. _____vision

Now try these

1. Copy the word. Use a dictionary to help write its definition.

   a) transaction
   b) transplant
   c) transform

   d) bicycle
   e) bilingual
   f) binoculars

   g) telephone
   h) telepathic
   i) telecommunication

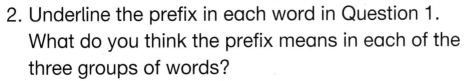

2. Underline the prefix in each word in Question 1.
   What do you think the prefix means in each of the
   three groups of words?

Common expressions

In our everyday lives we use many **common expressions** or **sayings**.

All's well that ends well.

Sometimes these **sayings** may be a little hard to understand!

The saying 'It's raining cats and dogs' really means it is raining hard.

Practice

1. Match these sayings to the pictures.

beat about the bush	have a bee in your bonnet
under a cloud	let the cat out of the bag
take the bull by the horns	give up the ghost

a) b) c)

d) e) f)

2. Choose two sayings from Question 1. Write what you think they really mean.

More to think about

Copy these sayings. Use the correct word from the box to fill each gap.

chickens	brave	fire	absence	job	waste	noise	more

1. _____ makes the heart grow fonder.
2. To put on a _____ face.
3. Empty vessels make most _____.
4. The _____ the merrier.
5. Out of the frying pan into the _____.
6. _____ not, want not.
7. When a _____ is worth doing, it's worth doing well.
8. Don't count your _____ before they're hatched.

Now try these

Match these sayings with their meanings.

to be a wet blanket	to refuse to take sides in an argument
to put the cart before the horse	to make little difficulties seem enormous
to sit on the fence	to be a spoilsport
to hang your head	to act while conditions are favourable
to strike while the iron is hot	to take punishment without complaint
to turn over a new leaf	to do things the wrong way round
to make a mountain out of a molehill	to get into trouble
to face the music	to be suspicious
to smell a rat	to make a fresh start
to get into hot water	to be ashamed of yourself

Suffixes (1)

A **suffix** is a group of letters added to the **end of a word** to **change its meaning** or the way it can be used.

Tariq is **ill**.
He has an **illness**.

The doctor needs to **treat** his illness.
She gives him **treatment**.

ill⟶ill**ness**

treat⟶treat**ment**

happy⟶happi**ness**

When the root word ends in **y** (sounding like **ee**), the **y** is changed to an **i** before adding the suffix.

Practice

Copy these words. Write the root word next to each one.

1. enjoyment – enjoy

2. fitness   3. pressure   4. encouragement

5. darkness   6. payment   7. business

8. failure   9. moisture   10. musician

11. architecture   12. magician   13. heaviness

More to think about

1. Copy the table. Write the abstract nouns in the box in the correct columns.

| laziness enjoyment happiness nastiness agreement |
| punishment excitement brightness |
| argument quietness encouragement goodness |

ment	**ness**

2. Add two more words to each column.

3. Use five of the above words in a short paragraph.

Now try these

ure	ian	ment	ness

1. Choose a suffix from the box to complete each word. Write the words.

   a) weak _____   b) depart _____   c) agree _____

   d) moist _____   e) fail _____   f) like _____

2. Choose a suffix from the box to add to each of these root words. Write the words.

   a) nasty   b) enjoy   c) pretty

   d) please   e) technic   f) furnish

Onomatopoeia

Onomatopoeia is when the **sound** of the word is **similar** to the **sound of the thing it describes**.

> Have fun reading this rhyme.
> It has many onomatopoeic words in it.

Jibber, jabber, gabble, babble,
Cackle, clack and prate,
Twiddle, twaddle, mutter, stutter,
Utter, splutter, blate…

Shout and shoot, gargle and gasp,
Gab and gag and groan,
Hem and haw and work the jaw,
Grumble, mumble, moan…

Chatter, patter, tattle, prattle,
Chew the rag and crack,
Spiel and spout and spit it out,
Tell the world and quack…

Beef and bellyache and bat,
Say a mouthful, squawk,
That is what some people do
When they merely talk.

Sniffle, snuffle, drawl and bawl,
Snicker, snort and snap,
Bark and buzz and yap and yelp,
Chin and chirp and chat…

Anon.

Practice

Write which animals these sounds remind you of.

1. Oink! Oink!

2. Quack!

3. Woof!

4. Buzz! Buzz!

5. Baa!

6. Miaow!

7. Gobble! Gobble!

8. Hiss!

9. Neigh!

10. Toowit! Toowoo!

More to think about

Write down what these sets of onomatopoeic words remind you of.

1. plip-plop, pitter-patter, splish-splash

2. stomp, trample, crunch

3. whoosh, zoom, roar

4. hiss, slither, slide

5. squish, squash, squelch

6. Pow! Zap! Thwaapp!

7. screech, groan, moan

8. rat-a-tat! knock-knock! ring-ring!

Now try these

> Make up your own if you like!

1. Write down four onomatopoeic words to describe each of these.
   a) the way different animals move
   b) the sounds of different insects
   c) the sounds of the wind
   d) kitchen sounds

2. Now try making up your own onomatopoem, like the one below, which tells a story through sounds only.

The Haunted House

Creep, creep, creep.
C R E A K!
Shhh! Hussss!
Tip-toe, tip-tap.
THUD! MOAN!
Grooaann!
Rittle-rattle.
SCREECH!
SMASH! CRASH!
Tiptaptiptaptiptap
Pant! Pant!
ZOOM!

> Choose one of these titles:
> The Woods at Night,
> A Storm at Sea or
> The Building Site,
> or make up your own.

# UNIT 10 Common letter strings

These words have the same **letter strings** but different **pronunciations**.

catalo**gue**

ton**gue**

Practice

1. Use the picture clue to find another word with the same letter string but a different pronunciation. Write the two words.

a) **find**

b) **echo**

c) **flow**

d) **guide**

e) **wallet**

f) **spine**

g) **over**

h) **cough**

More to think about

These words have common letter strings with different pronunciations.

Sort the words into three groups according to their common letter strings.

1. headache
2. mother
3. bough

bachelor

dough

both

tough

moustache

cloth

Now try these

Copy the words. Underline the odd word out in each set.

1. **thought** <u>drought</u> bought

2. **expensive** extensive alive

3. **loose** choose moose

4. **love** glove move

5. **eight** height weight

6. **flow** flower glow

Progress Test A

1. Write a synonym to match each word.
   a) wide   b) large   c) warm   d) worried
   e) hit   f) tiny   g) fasten   h) shout

2. Copy the table. Write five words in each column.

soft **c**	soft **g**

3. Copy the sentences. Use a different adverb to fill each gap.

   a) "Catch the ball," Ben called _____.

   b) "This soup has a fly in it," complained Mr Thomas _____.

   c) "Are you awake?" whispered Tessa _____.

   d) "Stop the dog barking!" Mum shouted _____.

4. Write each of these words in its plural form.
   a) puppy   b) zebra
   c) wolf   d) donkey
   e) seal   f) giraffe
   g) fish   h) bull

5. Copy these words. Underline the root word from which each
   comes. Add another word that uses the same root word.
   a) inform   b) autograph   c) uncover
   d) television   e) colourful   f) disappear

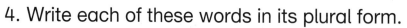

6. Copy the sentences. Underline the prefixed words.
   a) The sailor planned to circumnavigate the world.
   b) The postman rode his bicycle.
   c) Richard used the telephone to call the police.
   d) Mrs Caine needed a heart transplant.

7. Write down what these common expressions mean.
   a) To put on a brave face.
   b) When a job is worth doing, it's worth doing well.
   c) Absence makes the heart grow fonder.
   d) Waste not, want not.

8. Copy these words. Underline the suffix in each word.
   a) technician   b) enjoyment   c) pressure
   d) departure   e) nastiness   f) magician

9. Write some onomatopoeic words that represent:
   a) a horse walking down a road
   b) a clock
   c) a chicken
   d) leaves blowing in the wind

10. Circle the odd word out in each set.
    a) daughter   caught   laughter
    b) mallet   wallet   pallet
    c) tough   through   rough
    d) wine   spine   engine

UNIT 11 Figures of speech: similes and metaphors

A **figure of speech** is the use of words in a special way to create a **new or unusual meaning**.
Similes and **metaphors** use **figurative language**.

Tom is **as** quick **as** a flash of lightning.

When my Dad gets angry he is **like** a bull in a china shop.

A **simile** is when one thing is compared to another by using the words **as** or **like**.

The digger was a dinosaur with a huge, gaping mouth, and sharp teeth.

The wind is a giant's hand, pushing and snatching.

A **metaphor** is when you describe something **as if it were something else**.

Practice

Match the beginnings and endings of these well-known similes.

as sly as a	bat	as flat as a	cucumber
as blind as a	eel	as hard as	lead
as brave as a	bee	as heavy as	iron
as busy as a	fox	as light as a	pancake
as slippery as an	lion	as cool as a	feather

More to think about

Match each phrase with an appropriate metaphor.

a skyscraper at night	a vacuum cleaner	a foggy day
a cat screeching	an aeroplane	a tree
a goldfish swimming	a banana	

1. a giant with a hundred eyes
2. an iron bird
3. a bent, yellow boomerang
4. a wheel that needs oiling
5. an old man's white beard
6. amber traffic light in the rain
7. a green hand, reaching for the sky
8. an angry monster, sucking and roaring

Now try these

1. Make up some of your own similes. Copy and finish these in your own words.

   a) My hair is _____.

   b) A letter box is _____.

   c) A hedgehog is _____.

2. What could be described as:

   a) flat as a pancake?

   b) heavy as lead?

   c) light as a feather?

3. These riddles are metaphors. Can you answer them?

   a) I am an elephant's head.
      I squirt water on the flowers
      with my trunk.

   b) I give off light, but I'm not a lamp.
      I melt, but I'm not a lolly.
      I disappear when you use me.

   c) What being goes on four legs in the morning,
      Two legs in the afternoon,
      And three legs in the evening?

Homophones

Homophones are words that **sound the same** but are **spelt differently** and have **different meanings**.

Aman **rowed** past a man who **rode** his horse
on the side of the **road**.

Practice

1. Copy the sentences choosing the correct homophone for each.
   a) The (bow/bough) of the tree hung low under the weight of the snow.
   b) Susie wasn't sure (witch/which) was her jumper.
   c) There was a (creak/creek) as the door swung open.
   d) The (hare/hair) ran across the field.
   e) The tired travellers were pleased to see the (in/inn) where they could stop for the night.
   f) The (whole/hole) family were looking forward to their summer holiday.

2. Copy, from above, the homophone you haven't used in each sentence. Write a sentence for each one.

More to think about

1. Copy the sentences. Choose the correct homophone from the box to fill the gap.

there	their	they're

a) David and Louise were going to _____ Nan's house for Christmas.

b) _____ are the keys we have been looking for!

c) Have you got _____ telephone number?

d) _____ going to get in trouble if they do that!

e) _____ dog fell off the boat and was soaked.

f) At the fair _____ were lots of exciting rides.

g) _____ going to bed in half an hour.

2. Write a sentence for each word.

a) there   b) their   c) they're

Now try these

Copy the words. Write a homophone to match each word.

1. weight   wait
2. weather
3. meet
4. four
5. new
6. prey
7. pale
8. rain
9. sleigh
10. two
11. blue
12. fair

Borrowed words

English is a **living language**. Over the years we have **borrowed** many words from the languages of **other countries**.

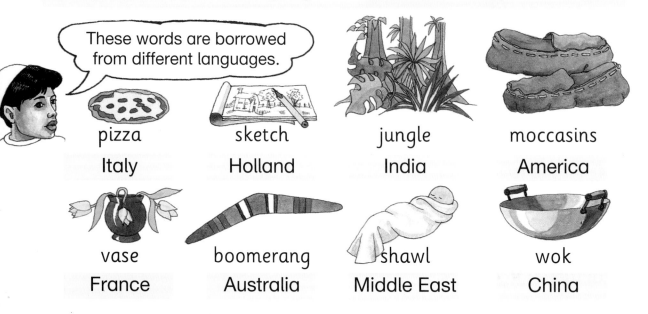

These words are borrowed from different languages.

| pizza | sketch | jungle | moccasins |
| Italy | Holland | India | America |

| vase | boomerang | shawl | wok |
| France | Australia | Middle East | China |

Practice

Here are some words we have borrowed from the Netherlands.

| deck | dock | easel | smuggle | skipper | sketch |
| | schooner | yacht | landscape | hoist | |

1. The Dutch were great sailors. Write the words that are connected with the sea or ships.

2. The Dutch had some great artists. Write the words that are connected with painting.

3. Write the words containing:

   a) ck   b) sk   c) ch

More to think about

Here are some words we have borrowed from Italy.

spaghetti	pizza	volcano	piano	ravioli	opera
umbrella	confetti	pasta	studio	macaroni	solo

1. Many Italians love food! Write the words connected with food.

2. Many Italians love music. Write the words connected with music.

3. Write the words that:
   a) end with **a**
   b) end with **i**
   c) end with **o**
   d) contain a double consonant

Now try these

Here are some words borrowed from other countries.

caravan bungalow boomerang cotton toboggan restaurant banquet blizzard ballet pyjamas moose zero boutique cafe shampoo kangaroo

Key:

Middle East

India

America

Australia

France

1. List the countries. Match the appropriate words to each.

2. Choose two words from each country. Write a sentence for each word to show you know the meaning of the word.

Spelling rules

Learn these **spelling rules**.

fly ⟶ flies

fly ⟶ fly**ing**

When adding a **suffix** to a word ending in **y** that follows a consonant, change the **y** to **i** (except for the suffixes **ing** and **ly**).

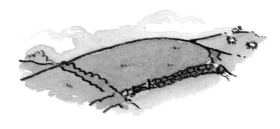

f**ie**ld

c**ei**ling

Put **i** (when it makes the sound **ee**) before **e** except after **c**.

Practice

1. Add the suffix in brackets to these words. Write the word.
   a) carry (ed)   =   carried
   b) funny (est)   c) enjoy (ment)   d) chilly (er)
   e) lazy (ness)   f) silly (est)   g) marry (ed)

2. Write the word. Separate the word into the root word and suffix.
   a) luckiest   =   lucky + est
   b) prettier   c) cloudiest   d) shyly
   e) smelliest   f) drying   g) naughtiness

More to think about

1. All these words have the letters **ie** or **ei** missing.
   Write the words filling the gap.

   a) ach _____ ve   b) r _____ n   c) f _____ ld

   d) l _____ sure   e) _____ ght   f) rec _____ ve

   g) bel _____ ve   h) th _____ r   i) c _____ ling

2. Check the words in your dictionary. Correct any mistakes.

3. Use five of the words above in sentences of your own.

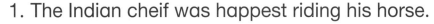

Now try these

Check these sentences. Write them out again, correcting any spelling mistakes.

1. The Indian cheif was happest riding his horse.

2. The soldier held his sheild above his head.
   It felt heavyer by the second.

3. Rachel beleived her brother had the smellyest socks!

4. The teacher wanted a reciept for the paiment of the coach.

5. When Afaq took thier golden retreiver to the vet, the dog
   was even naughtyer than on his last visit.

6. When Sonia's sister got married, Sonia thought she was
   the prettest and luckyest bride ever.

7. "Today is the chillest day of the summer this year,"
   reported the weatherman.

8. Mukta was luckyer than William. She recieved a huge
   bag of sweets.

Dialect words

In **different areas** of the country some people have **different ways of saying the same things**. This use of words or grammar is called a **dialect**.

This is how some people in different areas might say, "He's just a small boy."

He's just a we'an.
Scotland

He's just a nipper.
London

He's just a lad.
Lancashire

A dialect is different from an **accent**, which is to do with the **way we pronounce words**.

Practice

1. Copy this verse from a poem which uses a Black English dialect.

> Barry get a big bag,
> Barry climb de gate,
> Barry granny call 'im,
> But Barry couldn' wait.
> Im wan' get ova dere, bwoy,
> Before it get too late.

2. Copy the same verse in Standard English. Put the lines in the correct order.

> Barry's granny called him,
> Before it got too late.
> Barry climbed the gate,
> He wanted to get over there, boy,
> Barry got a big bag,
> But Barry couldn't wait.

More to think about

I'm just calling my trouble and strife on the dog and bone.

1. Many Cockneys in London talk in a dialect called **rhyming slang**. Match the words with their meanings and write them out like this: dog and bone = telephone

a)

dog and bone	wife
apples and pears	head
plates of meat	telephone
trouble and strife	feet
skin and blister	teeth
lump of lead	hair
Barnet Fair	sister
Hampstead Heath	stairs

b)

mince pies	road
Cain and Abel	boots
frog and toad	money
sugar and honey	knees
round the houses	eyes
bread and cheese	tea
daisy roots	table
Rosie Lee	trousers

2. Make up six sentences containing some words in rhyming slang.

Now try these

Build your own dialect dictionary. Copy these words and their meanings as a starting point.

Dialect word	Meaning
aye	yes
baffies	slippers
bairn	small child
banger	old car
daps	plimsolls
fainites	truce – "I give up"
mardy	spoilt
scarper	run away
scoff	eat
tatties	potatoes
wee	little

To start with, think of words which mean good or bad. There are often lots of dialect words to do with children, the weather, transport and food.

Unstressed vowels

Say these words aloud.

chocolate

vegetables

cupboard

When these words are said aloud the **vowels** in bold **are hard to hear**. These are called **unstressed vowels**.

Practice

Copy the words. Circle the unstressed vowel.

1. company
2. interest
3. freedom
4. temperature
5. portable
6. cupboard
7. business
8. factory

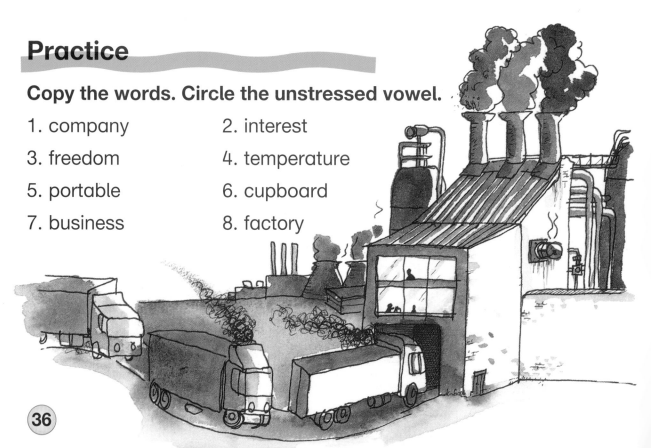

More to think about

1. Copy these words. Underline the word in each pair that has an unstressed vowel.

   a) tomorrow   gardener

   b) broken   princess

   c) refresh   valuable

   d) swimming   breakfast

   e) nursery   middle

   f) history   remember

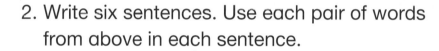

2. Write six sentences. Use each pair of words from above in each sentence.

Now try these

1. Copy these sentences. Each sentence has a word with an unstressed vowel missing. Underline the words that are spelt incorrectly.

   a) The diamond ring was valuble.

   b) The young childrn played in the sandpit.

   c) The team captin was excited when his team scored.

   d) The case of the disappearing P.E. bag was a mystry.

   e) "Don't forget your camra," called Mum.

2. Write the correct spellings for the words you underlined. Check your spellings in a dictionary.

Shortening words

We sometimes **shorten** words in different ways:

> It can't be ten o'clock already!

> Shall we go for a bus ride or do our maths?

> She is an important MP.

by **leaving out letters**

can<u>no</u>t = can't
ten <u>of the</u> clock = ten o'clock

by **leaving out suffixes or prefixes**

<u>omni</u>bus = bus
math<u>ematics</u> = maths

by using **abbreviations**

<u>M</u>ember of <u>P</u>arliament = MP

Practice

1. Match the contractions in Set A with their longer forms in Set B, like this: isn't = is not.

Set A	isn't	she's	I've	you'll	they'd
	I'm	don't	we're	who's	it's
	o'clock	shan't	Hallowe'en	how's	where've

Set B	I have	they would	it is	we are	I am
	she is	you will	who is	do not	is not
	shall not	where have	of the clock	how is	All Hallows Eve

2. Now underline the letter or letters that have been left out in each phrase, like this: isn't = is n<u>o</u>t

More to think about

Rewrite these sentences. Use the shorter form of the underlined words from the box.

cycle	fridge	phone	hippo	rhino	photo
	exam	miss	pram	zoo	

1. The lady took a <u>photograph</u> of the baby in the <u>perambulator</u>.
2. The <u>telephone</u> rang while I was getting a drink from the <u>refrigerator</u>.
3. <u>Mistress</u> Smith said I did well in the <u>examination</u>.
4. Which is bigger – a <u>hippopotamus</u> or a <u>rhinoceros</u>?
5. I went on my <u>bicycle</u> to visit the <u>zoological gardens</u>.

Now try these

Rewrite these sentences using the correct abbreviations from the box.

USA	UNO	CD	MP	Dr	km/h	CID	v	JP

1. I saw the Arsenal <u>versus</u> Chelsea football match.
2. He drove the car at well over 80 <u>kilometres per hour</u>.
3. <u>Doctor</u> Jones comes from the <u>United States of America</u>.
4. The purpose of the <u>United Nations Organisation</u> is to safeguard world peace.
5. I bought a <u>compact disc</u> of my favourite band.
6. Mrs Currie used to be a <u>Justice of the Peace</u> but now she has been elected as our <u>Member of Parliament</u>.
7. The detective was from the <u>Criminal Investigation Department</u>.

Prefixes (2)

When added to a word, the prefixes
in, **im** and **ir** often make its **antonym**.

```
6+5 = 11 ✓        4×6 = 24 ✓
7+5 = 12 ✓        3×7 = 21 ✓
8+5 = 13 ✓        7×15 = 105 ✓
6-5 = 1 ✓         8÷2 = 4 ✓
8-5 = 3 ✓         9÷3 = 3 ✓
10-5 = 5 ✓        10÷5 = 2 ✓ good
```

correct

```
6+5 = 12 ✗        8÷2 = 2 ✗
7+5 = 13 ✗        9÷3 = 4 ✗
8+5 = 14 ✗        10÷5 = 5 ✗
                  see me
```

incorrect

When you add a **prefix** to a word, you don't
change any letters, you **just add** the prefix.

An **antonym** is a word **opposite**
in meaning to another word.

Practice

**Copy the table. Put the words from the box into the
correct columns.**

| inability | irresponsible | imperfect | invaluable |
| irrelevant | inexpensive | impatient | irregular | impossible |

in	im	ir

More to think about

1. These words have the wrong prefix or are misspelt.
   Write them correctly.

   a) ireplaceable   b) inpatient   c) imaccurate

   d) inpossible   e) innexpensive   f) innconvenient

   g) iresponsible   h) imsufficient

2. Check the words in your dictionary.

3. Write three sentences, each using a word from above.

Now try these

1. Match the word to its definition.

patient	fairness
rational	able to do something well
justice	prepared to wait for something
competent	sensible and clear thinking

2. Write the antonym to each word.

3. Write four sentences, each using one of the antonyms.

Using a dictionary

You can use a **dictionary** for finding the **meanings** of **words** and **checking** their **spelling**.

Plurals are given.

This word has more than one meaning.

'n' stands for noun, 'adj' for adjective and 'v' for verb.

| bunch | buy |

bunch bunches (n) A bunch is a group of things together.

burgle burgles burgling burgled (vb) If you burgle a property you break in and steal things. burglar (n) burglary (n)

business businesses
1 (n) A business is a place of work.
2 (n) Your business consists of matters which concern you only.

busy busier busiest (adj) If you are busy you have a lot of things to do.

buy buys buying bought (vb) When you buy something you get it by paying for it.

Guide words tell you the first and last word on the page.

Additional linked words are given.

Different forms of the verb are given.

Practice

Write your answers using the page of the dictionary above.

1. The first word on the page is _____ and the last word is _____ .

2. The words are arranged in a_____ o_____ .

3. Write whether these words are nouns, verbs or adjectives:
   a) burgle   b) busy   c) buy   d) bunch   e) burglary

4. Which word means to have a lot of things to do?

5. What is the plural of   a) bunch? b) business?

More to think about

1. Write each set of words in alphabetical order.

    a) several   season   sewer   sequence   settle

    b) petal   pillar   pest   pill   pink

    c) cargo   caravan   caribou   cartoon   carpenter

    d) confess   consent   conduct   conceal   cone

2. These words are spelt incorrectly. Check them in a dictionary and write them correctly.

    a) definate (certain)

    b) forain (from another country)

    c) seperate (apart)

    d) neihbour (someone next to you)

    e) exiteing (thrilling)

    f) proffesor (a teacher at a university)

    g) goverment (those who govern)

    h) pecooliar (strange)

Now try these

Use your dictionary to help you.

1. Write a definition for each of these words.
   a) an album   b) a biography   c) a directory   d) a register

2. Write down who or what would live in these places.
   a) a monastery   b) barracks   c) an eyrie   d) an aviary

3. Write the difference between the words in each pair.
   a) root, route   b) bough, bow
   c) cereal, serial   d) sow, sew

4. Write two different meanings for these words.
   a) bulb   b) capsule   c) lock   d) drive

Suffixes (2)

Some **nouns change to verbs** when the suffixes **ise**, **ify** or **en** are added.

Stuart wrote an **apology**.
He had to **apologise** for copying.

Remember, when the root word ends in **y** (sounding like **ee**), the **y** is changed to an **i** before adding the suffix.

Some **verbs change to nouns** when the suffixes **ion** or **ism** are added.

Meena wanted to **suggest** they met at the park.
She made the **suggestion** and everyone agreed.

When we add **ion** it is sometimes necessary to change other letters as well.

Practice

1. Add the suffix **ise**, **ify** or **en** to these nouns to make them verbs.

   a) advert   b) light   c) simply

   d) magnet   e) fossil   f) fall

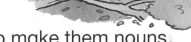

2. Add the suffix **ion** or **ism** to these verbs to make them nouns.

   a) pollute   b) reduce   c) special

   d) conserve   e) suggest   f) divide

More to think about

1. Write a sentence for each of these words to show its meaning.

    a) specialise   b) glorify   c) equalise

    d) solidify   e) quicken   f) lighten

2. Write the noun from which each word in Question 1 is made.

3. Write a sentence for each of these words to show its meaning.

    a) insulation   b) information   c) criticism

    d) opposition   e) suggestion   f) discussion

4. Write the verb from which each word in Question 3 is made.

Use a dictionary to help you.

Now try these

1. Copy these sentences. Underline the noun or verb that has been changed by adding one of the suffixes studied in this unit.

    a) The Frost family needed information about the city they were visiting.

    b) Laith didn't mean to frighten the bird.

    c) Nan's specialism is making fruit cakes.

    d) The teacher watched her class dramatise their version of the Romans invading Britain.

2. Write in brackets, after each sentence in Question 1, whether the word you have underlined is a noun or a verb.

3. Use these words in sentences of your own.

    a) criticism   b) quicken   c) discussion   d) glorify

Progress Test B

1. Copy these sentences. Circle the metaphors and underline the similes.

   a) When the lights went out Tuhil felt as blind as a bat.

   b) The snow was like a blanket covering the ground.

   c) The iron bird flew high in the sky.

   d) Dad slept as deeply as a hedgehog in hibernation.

   e) The hairdresser didn't know where to start on the wet mop.

2. Write a homophone for each word then put each homophone in a sentence.

   a) whether   b) two   c) slay

3. All these words are borrowed from Italy. Copy the words. Put in the final letter. What do you notice about all the final letters?

   a)

   pizz ____

   b)

   spaghett ____

   c)

   pian ____

   d)

   volcan ____

   e)

   umbrell ____

   f)

   oper ____

4. Spell these words correctly.

a) cieling b) lazyness c) cloudest d) thier

e) naughtyer f) liesure g) beleive h) dring

5. Match each dialect word with its meaning.

| little | old car | plimsolls | eat | yes | potatoes |

a) daps

b) tatties

c) wee

d) aye

e) scoff

f) banger

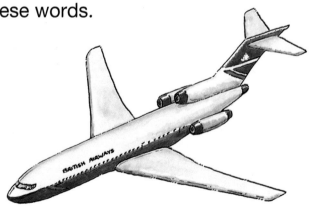

6. Circle the unstressed vowel in these words.

a) company b) regular c) interest

d) envelope e) freedom f) different

7. Write the abbreviations of these words.

a) British Airways

b) United Kingdom

c) World Wildlife Fund

d) miles per hour

e) Mister

f) Member of Parliament

8. Add the correct prefix to the words.

in	im	ir

a) _____ responsible

b) _____ expensive

c) _____ possible

d) _____ patient

9. Write these sets of words in alphabetical order.

a) alarm   air   allotment   album

b) regular   register   refuse   regret

c) workshop   woodworm   wound   wing

d) gravity   grass   grapefruit   grave

e) knight   key   knock   kilometre

10. Copy these words. Underline the suffix in each.

a) advertise   b) division   c) lighten

d) suggestion   e) criticism   f) solidify